THE FEEL-GOOD MOVIE OF THE YEAR

Luke Wright is a poet and theatre-maker. Flamboyant, political and riotously funny, Wright's inventive spoken word shows are enjoyed by thousands of people across the world every year. He is the author of two full poetry collections, three pamphlets and three verse plays. He is the winner of a Fringe First, a Stage Award and three Saboteur Awards. He lives in Suffolk with his two sons.

ALSO BY LUKE WRIGHT

POETRY

After Engine Trouble (Rough Trade Books, 2018)
The Toll (Penned in the Margins, 2017)
Mondeo Man (Penned in the Margins, 2013)
The Vile Ascent of Lucien Gore (Nasty Little Press, 2011)
High Performance (Nasty Little Press, 2009)

VERSE DRAMA

The Remains of Logan Dankworth (Penned in the Margins, 2020)
Frankie Vah (Penned in the Margins, 2018)
What I Learned from Johnny Bevan (Penned in the Margins, 2016)

NON-FICTION

Who Writes This Crap? (Penguin, 2007)

The Feel-Good Movie
of the Year

LUKE WRIGHT

For Koo

Penned in the Margins

LONDON

PUBLISHED BY PENNED IN THE MARGINS
Toynbee Studios, 28 Commercial Street, London E1 6AB
www.pennedinthemargins.co.uk

First published 2021

Printed in the United Kingdom by TJ Books Limited

ISBN
978-1-908058-86-7

CONTENTS

for KC

THE
Feel-Good Movie
OF THE
Year

Ex

We don't touch each other anymore;
twelve years in a double bed

down to business-like deals
we can't bring ourselves to shake on,

not even an x at the end
of a text. I'm not saying

that I want to. I just wonder
where we went. But today

you sent a photo of our son.
It stopped me as it flashed

across my palm. We were there.
In his face. In each other's arms.

A Pub Gig in the Middle of Nowhere

The locals take a pride in it:
no commerce down these silted
lanes. A coaching inn that's still

a coaching inn, fermented, sheltered
under hops and shouldering its centuries
with all the calm of village cricket —

blokes in whites and wives in hats
on yeasty afternoons. And I am here
to spin them all some yarns,

to tell them things they've known
for years and hope the way I do it
does the trick — an entertainment

older than this horse-brassed hearth.
And later, in the garden, I meet Daniel.
He'd sat there with his parents, sweet

and still, all through my show.
Seven years old, he tells me —
cherub almost rendered down

to boyhood and so much
like my own son, Sam;
a milk-faced storm

of cleverness and cheek
who comes at me now
with questions like weapons.

His father picks him up, blows
raspberries on his stomach,
sits him at their table with some chips

and rips the ketchup sachet. Wholesome
chores of parenthood! It's three nights
since I made a meal for mine.

And from the car park the fields
of the High Weald are endless.
In this middle of everywhere

I know the enormity of my choices,
the wretched, minute realness
of being lost at sea. I drive

back down the sunken roads,
tunnelled by trees beneath
a cold moon, and keep my boys'

car seats in the rearview. Empty now
and soon enough they'll go.
But I'll still witness boys like Daniel

pulling at a hand in Sainsbury's,
thwacking teaspoons on formica
in different, strip-lit M4 chains.

Perhaps those boys will haunt me.
Remind me of a time which I, through work
and through divorce, have cleaved

in two. Have taken half of.
Dear God. Only half.

Drawbridge

My poor old heart, I left its drawbridge down
all summer long, encouraged in the strangers.
Let them finger all my prize antiques,

inspect the mossy fridge and play the xylophone
of empties on the side. I left my journals
on the coffee table, certain pages marked

with betting slips. And nobody's been holding back.
What's the word for an orgy where everyone's
too fucked to fuck? This whole place reeks

of cum and ash and shame. What adult
holds a party in their heart
and broadcasts the address?

I suppose it's time to tidy up.
Raise the drawbridge, fill the moat
and gather wood for winter. Unless —

listen,
there's another way in.
Come with me.

The Lay-bys and Bypasses

The sun is up again in England and we've
just three strings on our violin, split ends
springing from the bow. We're coming down,

a dowager in a corridor clutching
a faded photo book, but listen now, I know
this place. Our song's still beautiful.

Let me recite for you, and tell you how
we're cast adrift from Europe, mad
upon the seas we claimed to rule.

Sat around the port, we shiver,
red coats threadbare at the elbows,
pith helmets a-brim with butts and sick.

Pray silence for my drunk thumbs. This is England.
And I can tell it like it is.
Last week I drove from Sheffield to Deal,

five hours without a stop (save pissing in a lay-by
outside Luton), my mind a-swim in caffeine pop.
I didn't use a map. Oh no! I know this place,

I thought, I know this place. But what exactly do
I know? The motorways? The lay-bys
and the bypasses? I lay-by. I by-pass.

There's life behind those conifers
that I will never see. I spit my wit
then split. I pinch myself to stay awake.

Two empty car seats in the back —
some days I just see skeletons. In a motor
they can't hear you if you scream.

So why not scream? I live the life
a wide-eyed child chose for me.
Perhaps you do as well? Rickety old

sleeper trains, we trundle on, we miss the points.
So here I am: another Poundland port town
a hundred miles from home,

watching seagulls swoop like stunt kites
on a coast that's not my own.
I try my best to make some sense of that.

I tally up the good days with the bad. I keep
my fires smouldering. I shovel on the poems
and the admin, the triumphs of my children.

I roll my terrors round my palm like Baoding balls:
the way the house feels after 9pm, the Christmas morning
lie-in, the gigabytes of smiles I dare not open.

Because I know what happy is: a carload
of friends on a festival weekend, a phone call
every night, drifting off with fingertips in touch,

tearing through the long grass with my boys, or standing
waist deep in September sea, gasping in the cold,
with lacerated lungs and a belly full of love.

That time I tumbled from a train in Taunton,
hungover and hilarious, it must have been
June, the sky was huge and blue.

I just adored it. So when it swallowed me,
I swallowed right back and down the hatch
went all of England with it. It knocked me

to my knees, singing: *Yes, I'm here.*
I'm here. The sky has not caved in,
the road is still beneath me and I'm breathing.

O, I claim to know this country. But all I do
is make it in my image: squeeze it into
spray-on jeans, file its teeth, distill its spleen,

take potshots at its pomposity for sport.
I love and loathe it as I love and loathe myself
and yes, I know it, because I know myself.

Spent

I have run out of goodwill for today.
Anxiety, that blowsy bully,
is perched on the sofa arm

stringing long globules of spittle
into my best brandy. And
this novel reads like a shopping list.

Tonight I won't admit I'm tired.
I'll pour myself another glass.
It's boring knowing how

to fix things. I'm going to wallow,
let my figures dip into the red.
You know me: never content

until I'm chucked down the steps
by the scruff of my neck, my bow tie
unravelling, like we did.

Lowestoft

I think I'll go to Lowestoft.
No, don't laugh, it's all right there —
paint flaking off the wooden fishing boats,

the statics watching from the Pakefield cliffs.
It's mostly sky
with just a little bit reserved for us —

a knee-deep sea and sand for miles.
I'll go there and I'll swim today. I'll sink
beneath the shallow waves

and let the silence gently crush my chest.
And afterwards I'll find a caff
and listen in to little bits of chat —

the foot-strut split and yod-drop
of this place. I'll net their thoughts
like butterflies: their heartbreaks and their wants,

their bellyaches. I bet I don't hear Brexit
mentioned once. I knew a man that let the news
consume him. He shouldered all that misery

as if it were his own. He shut out rooms,
disbarred himself from tables of his friends,
licked tin-foil sheets and stuck them on his windows.

Then, languishing in laptop light,
a breathless search for bullish blogs
to prove each cranky theory right —

and sometimes he was right
and righteousness
would flood the screen that night.

After Engine Trouble

I kept apologising for the car.
It wasn't my fault, but I knew you were tired
and Olive had school in the morning.
Even after all these months

I have to remind myself that this
is something new. That you won't
roll your eyes at me and sigh,
as if you had thrown your life away.

You reached beneath the passenger seat,
produced a National Trust blanket
and a tube of Pringles, oh my love,
a wardrobe full of silver linings.

The AA man arrived like someone's dad,
blew into his hands and talked in bloke.
We paid two hundred quid and coughed
onto the carriageway, better off.

To Hail a Cab

I remember Dad, when I was little
and up to London for the day with Mum.
We'd meet him at his office after work,

on our best behaviour in the lobby
under austere oil paintings of bewhiskered dukes.
And he'd step out of the lift, pinstriped

and powerful, somehow taller than at home.
He'd take us to Spaghetti House and afterwards
stand on the kerb to hail a cab,

one hand thrust into the air as now,
beside my own limp boys in midday throng
outside the Science Museum, I do the same.

Right arm in the air, left around their shoulders,
his magic trick to extinguish the orange light.
And as it's snubbed out and the cab slows

to a stop, I let myself believe
it might yet have the same effect.

Prayer

In 1980s concrete parks my mother
found a place to watch. *I need to keep*

an eye on you, she'd say and so she'd sit
and swing her keys or turn a *True Life* paperback

as I fell through an inky pool of time
to lose myself. Her *eye on me*: a length

of twine around my toe to pull me back
for air. But I grew up, as we grow up,

and scorned her eye and burned the twine,
dived drugged and drunk in dirty pools of bass.

I wasn't lost. I had myself — and lungs
the size of concert halls. I had it all,

a stomach full of life and all these eyes
on me, an easy job, a wife:

I've finished, Miss, a smug glance
at the clock. I gazed down at my navel

as if it were the world. *I had myself.*
I had myself. So nothing much,

as it turns out: a twang of id, a shallow
scrape of man. It's just, these days,

I take my own sons to the park
like nothing's wrong.

I watch them play and say, *I'll keep*
an eye on you. And there are times

I cannot breathe to know they only
have *my* eye on them. This eye that darts

around. This brittle twine. And when I sit
on empty nights and hold my knees

to watch them sleep, or see myself
reflected in a screened call,

in debts that grow like Pigmyweed,
in callow words I barely mean

and sense there might be something ugly
deep down in my soul, I long

to feel an eye on me, a length of twine
around my toe again. So can you,

will you keep an eye on me,
and, should I need it,

pull me up for air?

Status Update

Just one more minute's screen time, please —
to check how long my screen time's been.

I can't settle. My brain's uninsulated
wires fizz under the floorboards, burn up
my thoughts like dust motes.

(Please, don't touch that Bakelite
switch. I think we need
to get a man in.) All these screens,

these grim receipts of status spiked
on cluttered desktops
in my mind. Today

I spent three hours watching e-ink
notepads being unboxed. I learned
third-hand a well-known racist

commentator said a racist thing,
then scrolled until
I found the thing and dived

below the line, let outrage bleach
the gutters of my mind.
I've heard the brain

is wider than the sky. Well,
the skies round here are huge
and grey and I have nothing

to say. I have rendered every
stunning vista into
wallpaper. I used to think

that cynics were the clever ones,
their treadmill, low-fat cynicism
that sees the fault in everything

before they try to reel you in.
But cynics don't just see what's wrong —
they accept it. I don't know

what I want, can't picture myself
twenty years from now. I'm hasty
thumbs, erroneous corrections,

fidgeting the flesh clean off
my bones, a phatic vocal tic,
the ground floor of a tower block.

All that weight.

Clocks

Condemned to office work
in London, your workshop
was your weekend refuge:

the thick smell of machine
grease; corkscrews of brass filings
on the lino; and against the window

that colossal lathe, the colour
of steel warships. Out of this
industrial den emerged

the skeleton clocks you made
from intricate Georgian designs,
a hundred perfect bits

machined in brass and kept
under the glass domes
you'd wear white gloves to lift

each Sunday night, when you'd
deftly wind each tricky
mechanism. And every January

you put them forward
at the Model Engineer's Exhibition.
Once I fought to stay awake

to see you when you came home late.
You crept into my room
to uncase the gold medal

you had won and whispered
Pretty good eh?
You let me in. And though

I never found the knack
for making things
or helping in the workshop,

I learned from you the pride
that comes from skill.
And it's your clocks

that come to mind now
as I walk slowly
through the cardiac wing,

past doorway after doorway, framing
grey-skinned men, balding
and babyish in hospital gowns left

open at the chest, like shirts ripped
in bar fights, almost missing you,
so haggard with the IV in your arm —

the clocks. I think about the clocks
you filled our house with, years ago,
when we had all that time.

Sent Out, Aged Ten

I had it coming: one comedy recorder squeak
too many. I shrugged and sauntered out,
a cocky streaker with a copper's helmet, waving
at my classmate crowd. But on the flagstones

outside the door it felt like getting stripped
for swimming with the year above, as
wafting from the dinner hall came
the suet-cabbage smells of lunch. And then

the only thing I dreaded more: Mrs Williams.
I shrank into my shoulders but of course
she clipped across to me: *Oh Luke,*
sent out again! And that was all it took

to torch the rafters of my heart and bring
the whole lot down — the falling grades
and bullying — the old familiar eye sting.
And as I wept, ashamed, she scooped

and cradled me — my almost adolescent bones.
I still recall her satin blouse, her breasts, and how
I almost let her hold me there before disgust
surged up and, writhing in her arms, I kicked free.

Clouds

I board the red-eye.
Sour-breathed and porcelain-faced,
shooting tired bile from my bony thumbs.

It's cosmic up above the clouds today:
proper, proper gorgeous
in that way that art can't match.

Don't try it at home, kids;
you'll just end up with screensavers,
an inbox full of Instapoems.

Oh yes! And I am filth against the blue
but who cares about me anyway?
I'm dissolving like an aspirin in the clear lake of the sky.

My Sadness

I wonder if I wanted this —
some low-dosage sadness,
a saline drip of sadness;
some nights alone
to pull my sadness
round my shoulders like the nylon blanket
the four of us would sit beneath to watch
Lovejoy on Sunday nights.

And yes, it hurts to see a wholesome family,
the children home for Christmas,
couples in their sixth decade,
wise and corduroyed,
who wear each other like shirts
saved for painting in.

But I think I wanted this —
to submit to my sadness like a pill,
to sink to my knees,
my arms above my head, singing:
O, Romantic sadness!

Vinyl sadness!
Longhand sadness!
Ink-blotted sadness!
Natural fibre,
slow-cooked,
hand-made,
analogue sadness!
Sadness
     in all its honest dust.

And now
I shall wear my sadness
to wear my sadness in,
ready for when my parents die
and my friends pull up their drawbridges,
for when my body rusts.

I am content to sink below its water line.
My sadness like a bath;
my sadness like the early aches of flu;
my sadness like my muscles after sport
or a good beating
before the bruises come up,
        before I hack my lungs,
           before the water goes cold.

Sophie

I began the day with your name, saw it
in the subject line and mistook you for the sender,
saved you till last, for something real, then

returning, realised my mistake, and somehow
knew, before I'd read the words, the sad,
unlikely news, like grey light through the curtains.

I don't know what to do with death
so kept you about my person as I brewed the tea,
cut sandwiches and chivvied my boys

from bed, remembering that you
have sons as well. Amid all this grief,
these multitudes of graphs, a single,

quiet tentacle has found its way
past my front door and I remember
now how grey the worst things are,

how much they steal our words, our energy;
precisely what we hoped might
get us through. But I must try to claw

some back, because I think
that's what you would have done.
Just last night my son told me how much

he loved his English teacher and I wished
she could have heard him talk. Now, sitting
in my car, outside my house, the engine

running, I imagine all the girls who must
have said the same of you. Those bright girls
you adjusted and turned around to face

the world, hundreds of them, scattered
into adulthood and opening a message
with your name.

Cast Photo

It's a nice school, this: single sex,
and science labs. And in the corridor
outside the black box theatre, photographs
of past productions that date back
to the '90s. Contemporaries of mine
in mulled *Macbeth*s and steamy *Streetcar*s

calling me across the fallen decades.
Here's a full cast shot of *Daisy Pulls It Off.*
All right then, a silly one, the teacher might have said.
Cue jazz hands, best friends goofing cheek to cheek.
Picture them: bright girls in Alice bands and dirndl skirts
who learned their lines out on the far end

of the playing field, making daisy chains. Back then
they might have taken any part. What became
of them, these scores of girls who line
the walls that stretch off
down this tapered
corridor?

Friend Request

Mate! To think you still exist; out there
now in hideous 4K clarity, logging onto
Zoom and catching up on Gogglebox
in the aluminium twinkle of an eco-bulb.
Don't you prefer the past? The world beneath
a vinyl crackle, its edges blurred, its phatic chatter
rendered down to poetry? I could leave you
there, suspended in the amber of a Polaroid,
where our parents, tweed-skirted and double-cuffed,
twiddle the cord of a rotary dial telephone
and smoke in the house. But then I think of
Calke Abbey, the nursery shut up the day
the little Lord inherited the master bedroom.
On the rug, a dinky car, abandoned
like a goblet at Pompeii. The tyranny of that.

The Rack

I am both: a single parent on the Brexit coast and
dumbstruck lover on Brighton's shingle shore

mad-rambling declarations in the mandy mist
of seafront clubs with glitter on my cheeks;

then fish fingers and chips for tea
next day, motorways apart, the spelling tests

and guided reading, lives and levels
on my vintage SNES. Me with my children,

you with yours — picking at the Snapchat
psychodramas, eating hearty stews, while

I read Philip Pullman books to my two in their beds —
Will and Lyra in their separate worlds.

And I wish each night that I could cut
a window in the air, slip through exhausted

neat into your arms then stumble back
when light creeps through the curtain crack

for Coco Pops and combed hair.
But love has put me on a rack

of straining tarmac stirrups
and thunderous white noise and sometimes

when the screws tighten in Dartford tailbacks
and I swear my skin will split, my bones pop

clean from their sockets, I worry what this rack
will do to me, if I'll limp all through my life.

I pray that I'll walk taller for the pain.
I work to count the sweetness of relief —

children tearing through the playground,
pouncing up at me, that smile of yours

that continent-wide smile of yours, as doggedly
I limp around the dog-leg of your stair.

A Piece of Quiet

for Aidan

At three you minced the phrase you'd heard us say.
You tugged my sleeve: *I need a piece of quiet.*

Later, we discovered you required this
much more than us. We learned your diagnosis

like the rosary. It helped us understand
how noise could flood your mind, taught us

how to better *cwtch* your anger, counselled us
that it was not our fault. Ten years

have passed. Our family's split but still
we share your gifts. You tug my sleeve

to escape the party's treble. We ditch
the trampoline park's dreadful keening,

hit the showers early at the pool
and go outside to let the sky unfold

above our heads, re-earth ourselves in clearings
and tear each other off a piece of quiet.

-

Merch Stall

for Sam

I sign the books and you collect
the cash. You're eight, as careful with money
as you are with love. Up and up it goes

as kind-eyed strangers hand you springy notes.
You tally up our profit in your head and whisper
it to me. When the bell rings

and our punters drift away I tell you
ten pounds is yours to keep.
I turn and gather up the books. You fall silent

for a moment, counting in your head. I'm about
to clip the case shut when you stop me,
hold the tenner out, ask if you can buy a book,

and break the bloody bank.

Tidal

I tried it on again last March
but you slapped me in the face
then cut me dead all April long.
By May we were exchanging
pleasantries and then a blazing
June arrived and I fell drunk

into your arms, your salty body
folding over mine. After that
I couldn't keep away, before and
after work, all through July, till
August came mercurial and strange
and every day I felt you growing cooler.

We worked at it through warm
September dusks but soon we were
reduced to quickies, fully clothed,
which felt the way it always does:
like constructive dismissal. All winter
now I've watched you from my car,

raging, foaming at the mouth, clutching
bottles, bodies, lashing out.
But I know you and how you
lapped my sandy feet. I know
one day you'll take me back,
and by the time we roll around
to March, I'll be aching for your slap.

O, the years they heap amendments on our instincts

and today on the bus Mark couldn't get over
the fact this girl had an M&Ms phone case,
an anthropomorphised sweetie with gloved jazz hands.
But WHY though? he kept saying.
And sure, I might have shrugged, but believe me

I get it: watching the English
is like watching your front lawn get trampled
on match day, like watching a drunk man
trying to roll a fag with your baccy
He keeps dropping the Rizla. *Here mate, hold my pint.*

Like a stag-do in the quiet carriage,
a fatberg of grown men in distressed jeans
lauding their superhero movies.
But DUDE this one is fucking DARK though. Oh, you think
I'm being uncharitable? You should have seen me

at Mark's age, screaming into paper bags
as if my rage would Cif me clean —
but the sweetest boy I ever met became
a hedge fund manager and I've got to keep
my coalition together.

It's just, right now, I have this feeling
of something trying to burst back out —
like a cage unclanking,
like the sky above the high street
turning gold then red then black.

Language

I'd take the escape ladder
down into the cooling tower
of my thoughts if it weren't
for all that burning steam
billowing at the top.

Monster

I've got a monster in me:
spats and tails,
and ridiculous jewellery. Fuck yes,
my monster can accessorise.

And this beautiful bastard is here
to sell the night to you!
Cocking his leg
to lube the chat.

Watch him dance on a soixante-quinze,
a double finger gun salute,
chest out, arms as wide as Christ:
    oi oi oi lads lads lads

Monster
diatribing like a columnist,
opinions like confetti
from an arsehole.

Oh, he's atrocious
but he knows it;
he called himself out
when he chose that shirt

and refused to do the buttons up.
You can't touch him
because he's already touching himself.
Monster. Monster.

And recently my monster's
been escaping every night.
I can't be arsed to latch the cage;
I thrill to hear its steel door clank.

Yes, this old screw has turned.
I thump my chest at five o'clock to wake him up.
Sun's over the yard arm, Monster;
grease your hair and ditch your sponsor.

The Monster's coming out!
    oi oi oi lads lads lads
The Monster's coming out!
The Monster's coming out!

Delighting in the tang of human skin
and swimming in the eyes of strangers —
he loves you all, he wants you all,
he wants to take you home with him, he wants to take you home.

But come the acid morning he'll be snoring,
grinning hard at some old filthy dream inside my chest
while I take tea with you,
afraid to ask.

Autumn

O, sting of cold October mornings,
bleak as car park COVID test sites,
here you are again, spring's wise cousin,
winter's henchman slapping a balled fist
into his palm, and with you fresh blazers
and undented pencil cases, sober evenings
from where I see just how the summer
sends me mad. I need these mists that sit
above the water meadows to remind me
nothing's clear. I need to wake
before the sun is up and reach out
for the light switch in the dark.

Just Look at Us Now

Pinched plasticine faces outside beige bricked municipal
places, sheltering from drizzle under fire escapes,
back doors bricked open, drinking in the smoke

the way on sunny days we *tap tap tap* our phones, chins down,
and let the blue turn grey above our heads, recognise
the clickbait, click-click on, and let the seconds slip away for good.

Here we are, voting for the fascists. *Yes sir! This tyranny
is such a breath of fresh air!* We canvass hard for Armageddon,
doorstep for our own impending doom, dream like eagles

and live like moles down holes, half-cut on glossy stories
where advertising slogans bloom like algae. We swipe
from happy ending to iconic closing shot, bathe

in its reflected solar light, refuse to let the thought
of darkness in; distract ourselves with zoos of memes, minutia
swapped like playing cards. Pigs can't raise their heads to look up

at the sky; even killer whales get the bends; and, contrary to popular belief, lemmings aren't suicidal. They simply have strong migratory tendencies: a need to get away and hang the cost, an ache inside,

that pulls them over cliffs.

The Other Poet

I see the other poet is a 'professional forager'.
Of course he is. Naturalist
by day and bard by night.
The utter bastard.

Imagine him — scrawling by the open fire:
the shepherd's pie; the glass of red;
the coarse, well-holed jumper.
Barbour hung and dripping on the flagstone.

No, not a Barbour —
something as efficient, but unbranded.
(It's me who owns the Barbour
for my infrequent country strolls.)

I bet he's never bitched about a shortlist
or massaged his Instagram.
I doubt he'd even heard about the prize,
the name of which is stickered on his book.

I doubt he even looked up, too busy
living a life not built on brag or self,
his every rumination fixed and anchored
in layers of rich and mulchy earth.

Now All That Shined is Shit

Some felon's sunk my sovereign sun inside his cloudy keks
and given me the slip. Today is doctors' waiting rooms

and dog shit on the dance floor. Today my heartache clings
to me like burs and everyone's an anti-vaxxer, a queue of cars

behind a tractor. O, today I'm thatch and Twitter is a tinderbox;
the slightest thing might set me off and I could take you all

down with me hissing. I'm arguing about Brexit on Reddit
and the lines I bellowed beaming from my handlebars just

yesterday are Brasso on my tongue. It isn't that it's raining yet;
it's knowing rain will come.

Fortieth

Early for the party I found
a Sam Smith's & ordered
a brandy & took it outside
& rolled a thin cigarette
& cadged a light from a Frenchman
& smoked as the ice turned
to water in the glass,
held in the palm of a Saturday
in Smithfields, an afternoon
as quiet as the click and crackle
of a needle on a record
after playing the first
movement of some splendid
symphony and willing me
to flip the disc
and play the other side.

Akrasia

Why can't I follow
my own good advice
and curve this

submissive urge,
on my knees again
in front of a box of

cigarettes, a tub of
ice cream, another
quiet week-night pub,

on my knees before even
you, my fingers interlocked:
are you my God?

Will everybody leave me? Do I want them to?

The opposite of addiction is connection.
I nicked that off Johann Hari but he
won't mind, he's been there. And y'know what,
maybe I'm all right just rattling, echoing one-liners
off walls of my own choosing. *How do you let go*
without giving up? This is the question
of the morning as I try to rusticate
my anxiety. Perhaps I'll get a few beers in,
sit on the sofa and watch some Yoga with Adrienne;
a little bit of neck hygiene goes a long way
and I've begun to talk to myself more kindly.
I bought some new trainers, read all the way
to the end of an article. It's true that 90%
of shit can be fixed by a long walk, so
pass me that sou'wester, watch me shuffle
beneath the rustle of the poplars. I think
it's all in the feel, like locating a vein, knowing when
to drop the bass, or finding the biting point.
Fuck me, those trees are keen. They're shooting up
round here like school boys' shins. Just look.

Reading for Pleasure

for Sam

And what pleasure it brings to me.
When I tuck you in you say,
Leave the light on, Dad, I want to read!

I forgot about you the other night.
You came back down at half past ten
with fizzy eyes: *I've finished it.*

Seconds, minutes, whole hours slip by
now words can hold you, steady
as a rock pool. The power of this,

of knowing you can exist within your solitude,
rely on no one but yourself. As if you knew,
that in the end, that's all you'll have.

I watch you turning pages, deaf to us,
each one a cautious step away
from me, leaning less and less,

and understand how one day
you will walk away for good
and know how beautiful that is.

And I Saw England

In dusty deep July I threw
my sun-scorched body in the Waveney,
cooled my blood against

the streamer weed and pennywort,
then breast-stroked up the river under
alder glades to turtle-bask

on a disused bridge support and gaze
at England in the water's pickle-green
and in the swan that glided

fifty yards upstream, attended by her
cygnet train, imagine England
in the centuries of blacksmiths' boys

and parlour maids who'd slid
their molten bodies off that bridge
on burnt-grass days like this.

And I saw England in the little
rowing boat and in the loosestrife flowers
and in the mighty cob that slipped

along the river top beneath the smudge
of butter sun towards me and his pen
and cygnets far beyond my back.

I kept an eye on him as I splashed off
to reach my clothes, my bit of bank,
but when I veered away he veered as well,

so I veered further still, convinced
that he would see I meant no harm.
I gave that cob the river's width

but still the beast bore down on me
till he was only inches off and then
his vast wings flapped, the white arm

of his neck rose up, his ancient orange eyes
flashed like fire on Boer farms, like mortars
dropped on Baghdad compounds.

I saw that stately mask slip as it did
on Belfast streets and flinched
as England's martial, murderous hiss

shot out at me from its serrated beak.

Bring Me My Devil

This virus saw my devil off and left me
in the tutelage of my best self who turns out to be
an archbishop, a haughty health fanatic,

a McEwan-smug lecturer in rimless half-moons,
hell-bent on teaching me the names of trees,
ruddy as a camper, marching me

across the April fields: *Look a tit!* Now life
is one long limber up in gym shorts
with a tidy hem. I'm wading through

a swamp of sourdough, playing chess
by second-class post, blinded by order, bleached
as pale as the concrete walls of a Soviet-era theatre.

God I miss my devil! Shitting like a
barn owl down my back, whispering his
slanders in my ear. You wouldn't catch him

clapping for the nurses or mucking in or queuing
for the Co-op. *Fuck no*. He'll be in some dive bar
now, out there in the shadowlands. Some place

beyond our squeaky comprehension.
But when they click the combination lock
and set us free, I'll send for him.

I'll drag him flailing from his cups
and dunk him in the horse trough.
I'll scream for him to do his worst:

line 'em up and get 'em out;
unspool my weeks of hearty labour;
piss on all the ledgers of my soul.

Oh, someone bring my devil back to me —
in the hot throng of leaking bodies,
in shared saliva, at rank urinals,

in dark basements thick with lockdown dust.
To rob me of my dreamless sleep.
To feed me saturated fats.

To mock me as I vomit on my boots
and push his horny thumbs
into my well-fed heart and pull.

Portcullis

It seems it's jammed, this lattice
grille of last resort. To all intents
I'm open now for business;

the drawbridge growing mossy
from the moat, the car park freshly
gravelled. I'm sure I'll have it raised up

in a moment. I'm doing everything
I can. I beg you, please be patient.
Why not use my interactive app?

Take a virtual tour, design a banner,
hang it in my virtual tiltyard. Trace
the journey of the stone that built me,

plundered from a foreign enemy
and heaved on skis by slaves; or read
about that final dreadful siege,

the moment the wrought iron
bent like tin and a band of looters
thundered in, upturning plan chests,

burning flags, the faithful dragged off
screaming from their shredders, marched
outside and shot against the wall.

We're Back at the End Again

Come and whimper, pot-bellied like a cuck.
Scroll through everything you know
you'll never have. Picture your partner happy,
shutting the door in your face. Let it
loop like a gif. Your child being thrown in the air
by the well-toned arms of a better man.
Your mother, drunk, shitting herself at sports day.
Go fixed-point gambling. Wank in the train toilets.
Go on, it's your birthday. Meet her
at a Shell garage on the South Circular
or the Burger King at Thurrock services
for a month of Tuesday evenings in November.
Finger each other like fifteen-year-olds,
bash teeth with morning breath, and talk about
the sofas you'll own in your 40s, your dream sofas,
your forever sofas, from which you'll submit your letter
to Graham Brady, have another donut, input
the calories, stare at the cracked fascia of your iPhone,
your eyes like the spirals of a vending machine,
straight to DVD, resentments ripening like tubercles.

Spend Easter Weekend with a dozen TV agents
and some bloke you assume to be their dealer.
Cheer up: Kit Harrington is on the One Show.
Hasn't he done well! Kit Harrington.
He was in that thing, you know, that thing.
Look at Kit Harrington. Plunder yourself for parts.
Snap that elastic band in the post office queue,
at parent's evening, in the flickering gloom
of the village film club. Julia Hartley-Brewer is here
with her strap-on. Go on. You know you want to.
You can be your own optimism; she'll be…
Julia Hartley-Brewer. Submit like you always do.
No one hates you, mate. No one's even noticed.
It's tailbacks for miles in both directions.
Feel the heft of your gut, the spot on your pubis.
Pull your ugliest face. Stare into the toilet bowl.
Smell the panic seeping from your armpits.
Submit to the sugar tax. Keep on glugging.
Run your tongue over furry teeth.
Picture yourself as a four-year-old,
squinting in the sunlight, holding a spade,
so unspoiled, so sweet. That's it. Just there. Good boy.

The Turning on the Halesworth Road

I observe it, private as a superstition,
in the chatter as we drive towards
the seaside sun. I'd barely know

my way down there these days.
The railway bridge, the high-banked
country lanes, the dogleg right,

the forecourt where we parked
our separate cars. I can't recall
the counsellor's name. I think

I hugged a cushion. You made good
use of the tissues. It didn't
work. We only went three times.

I guess I knew. My children shriek.
A hundred yards ahead of us,
directly in our sights, the black cross

of a crow pecks roadkill. *Dad!*
I tell them that she's fast, she'll be okay, but
when she flies off Aidan turns to me:

We hit one once. Remember that?

ACKNOWLEDGEMENTS

I'd like to thank my editor, publisher and friend, Tom Chivers. The middle ground we meet upon has become a place of outstanding natural beauty.

Acknowledgements are due to Nina Hervé of Rough Trade who published earlier drafts of 'Prayer', 'The Lay-bys and Bypasses' and 'After Engine Trouble' in *After Engine Trouble* (Rough Trade Books, 2018); to Hugo Williams, who published 'Ex' in *The Spectator*; and to Dan Clayton, who commissioned 'Bring Me My Devil' on behalf of the English and Media Centre. 'After Engine Trouble' was the result of a speed-writing session with John Osborne.

I'd also like to thank my pals Nick, Kate and Molly, who have all listened to me read early drafts of some of these poems. And to dear old Martin Rowson, who kept a careful eye on me during lockdown and publicly goaded me into writing more.

Thank you to my family: Mum, Dad, Olive, Sam, Aidan and, especially, my dear love, Rosy, who is able to edit out my more mawkish lines at 3am on a big night out.

Finally I would like to thank Kate Clanchy for her passion, generosity and ability to swat a gerund at fifty paces. Thank you, Kate, for all the help you have given me. This book is dedicated to you.